Surviving Hard Times

a Livingbook

I0474038

Patricia Renard Scholes

Dedication

This book is dedicated to all those who refuse to let others dictate how they are to survive. We are not helpless. Neither are we violent. We are independent, and we are survivors.

Acknowledgments

Blessings to my children who, through hard times, taught me what was important.

Table of Contents

Introduction

(written originally in 2012, updated 2016)

When the housing market crashed, followed by the stock market, some of us wondered what we had lost in savings and investments. Others worried about their retirement income. Many lost more than investments and retirement income based on investments. Many lost their jobs, then their homes, then their courage.

What do you do when it's all gone?

2016 note: No matter what we're told, most of us know that very little has changed. In fact, much has become worse. Financially, the best thing you can do is get out of debt.

This is not a book about investments or wise places to put your money. I wrote this book to offer encouragement to those who lost nearly everything. I wrote this book for you, those of you who desperately want hope. I write from experience, my own and the experience of others. You will find these chapters spiced with stories of courage, sacrifice and even failure and defeat. But know that no matter the failure or the sin, God forgives, even before we've done anything right to show him.

2106 note: Half of this book contains recipes. Some of these foods will not be available to you, especially as times get worse. Learn to substitute. Learn to use the food God has given you, and be grateful. This is the most important lesson you can learn.

I make no apology that this book reflects a solid faith in God. I have been through, and survived, economic upheaval. I could not have done so without a deep abiding faith in God, my Father, who sent Jesus, my Savior and my friend, who made the way to the Father accessible. Did I go through my own story perfectly? Of course not. Otherwise I would never need a Savior. This book is written from my human, often frail, standpoint, while I grasped the hand of a holy God. God never let go of me. He will never let go of you either. Take heart! No matter what happens, one thing is certain. God loves you too much to let go of you. You *will* get through this.

2016 note: There are government-sponsored programs, which are important. But you need to remind yourself that as things get worse, they will be abandoned. The elite will make sure they live well, eventually at your expense. Constantly remind yourself that there will come a day when the government programs will end. Prepare yourself for that, if you want to survive, of course.

A reminder: All our social programs began first in the Church (I mean the universal Church, not any one specific denomination). These days we expect our government to do what we, as Christians, began. It's time, Christians, to pick up the slack. We cannot continue to expect a man-made system to do our work for us.

The bottom line, if you did not pick up this book because you are barely making it, then at least consume less so that you can give more. Giving is a necessary part of our faith.

Chapter 1

Making Ends Meat
A Guide to Meatless, or Nearly Meatless, Meals

My daughter Min, while growing up, often heard the term: *making ends meet.* Considering that meat was a luxury in our diet, she heard "making ends *MEAT*," which she interpreted as a meatless meal made at the end of a paycheck. Although she now knows what we meant, she still needs to process the phrase, an act that her husband finds humorous.

People *need* several things (not necessarily in this order), a home, food, clothing, the love of their family, and a relationship with their Creator. The first thing that seems to go out the window during a time of crisis is adequate food. The rent or mortgage gets paid. Maybe the car loan gets paid. Maybe some of the creditors get their share. But because the grocery budget is more flexible, we often cut into it to pay another bill, and hope next month will be better.

All right, let's cut into the grocery budget, but let's eat well, too.

First of all, meat is a luxury, not a necessity. Am I a vegetarian? Certainly not! The definition of a vegetarian is "lousy hunter." But I know the difference between a need and a strong desire. We don't *need* meat. The human body, unlike our cats and dogs, functions quite well without it. Cats and dogs need meat to get essential proteins. Without meat, they will go blind. Humans, unlike our carnivorous friends, manufacture certain amino acids that theirs don't. We can get the remaining amino acids from certain food combinations.

A Complete Protein

Have you ever wondered why you put milk on cereal? It tastes good. Yes, but it's more than that. Milk and cereal make a complete protein.

Let's put it like this:

Any milk product and any cereal product (or potato) make a complete protein. Examples:

- Cereal and milk.
- Macaroni and cheese.
- Scalloped potatoes with or without cheese.
- Bread pudding.
- Potatoes with cream gravy.
- Cheesy rice.
- Potato soup.
- Rice pudding.

Eggs are nearly a complete protein. They only need a bit of help:

- Eggs and cheese.
- Eggs and toast.
- Huevos Rancheros.
- Egg sandwiches.
- Breakfast burritos with egg and potato filling.

Legumes, such as dried peas, lentils, and beans with any grain or milk product make a complete protein. Such as:

- Beans and tortillas.
- Beans and rice.
- Pea soup made with milk.
- Lentil stew and fresh-baked bread.
- Butterbeans and cheese.
- Black-eyed peas and cornbread.

Of course, the price of everything, including beans and especially milk, has gone sky high. So we have some alternatives. Use powdered milk. Ugh! Yuck! Nasty! All right, I know how powdered milk tastes. It tastes like…um, powdered milk. Powdered eggs taste even worse. If you ever run across any, either run the other direction, or put them in as part of the ingredients in your meal. You'll be sorry if you reconstitute them for scrambled eggs some morning. But if you reconstitute powdered milk and use it only for cooking and save that good 1% or 2 % for drinking, you have cut your grocery bill, and have not sacrificed nutrition.

2016 note: We are now seeing boxed milk that you put with your canned goods, which doesn't taste too bad on cereal, especially after refrigeration. As our ability to buy groceries diminished (we're on Social Security), we started going to the food bank (after three years of no milk and limited cheese). I do wonder, however, at the nutrition in boxed milk.

A note on fruits and vegetables: vitamin pills don't really work that well. You really need to eat fruits and vegetables. So add them every chance you get to your meals. I know, they're almost as expensive as meat, but they're necessary.

Regarding snack foods: avoid them. Most are non-food items. They are worse than an unnecessary luxury. They add very little food value, and steal vital nutrition from the good foods you've just eaten. Such items (I hate to call them foods, because that's the last thing they do—feed you) include, but are not limited to:

- Most chips, especially the greasy fried chips.
- All soda, especially sugar-free sodas.
- High sugar anything, including cereal.
- High sodium snacks.

And, of course, those are what we crave. But if you want to eat well, and your budget is limited, make sure you buy only good foods first. The above are luxury items. Indulge when you have a bit of extra to spend. By the way, be grateful for luxuries. Give thanks when you are able to buy them.

We may be going through a financial crisis, but our infrastructure is solid. Our government still stands. Public transportation, although more expensive than it used to be, still functions. Sanitation crews still work. Most of our water is potable. These are things that much of the rest of the world has never seen. We really need to be grateful for living in a country where potato chips are accessible luxuries, and clean water is practically a given.

A Note on Water

Not everyone in this country has access to potable water. I live in a desert. Those who ranch in this desert put huge water tanks on the beds of their trucks to haul water for themselves and their livestock.

I used to live in a campground in a forest by a creek. Because the owners of the campground lived in Texas, they didn't understand that the cheap plastic waterlines they put in for their summer guests could not survive a winter.

Each winter the lines froze and we, who lived there year round, had no water. So we went into town to a gas station where we filled every bottle, jug, jar and pitcher with water for cooking and bathing. During that time the runoff ditch next to our trailer ran with clear mountain snowmelt. So I stuck a five-gallon pickle bucket into the flow of water and used that to fill my washing machine. The machine still worked, just the water line didn't.

My point is, people who are survivors make do. They find ways to get around a system that is inconvenient or sometimes even hostile. Eating right means you must have a *clean* water source. All the complete proteins in the world won't help you if your water is unsanitary. Boil it if necessary. Drive the twenty miles into town to get it if necessary. Do whatever you can to keep yourself healthy, because YOU are the best resource to provide what your body needs. A system can't do that for you. You must be invested in living well, despite your circumstances, and sometimes despite your government.

Mostly Meatless Recipes

Most of these are "scratch" recipes, meaning they use no, or limited, canned or packaged products. Making a meal from scratch costs extra time but saves you money. So if your time is short, you may need to adjust the recipes to fit your current situation.

These recipes are my own, and they are few because this is not primarily a cookbook. But if you want really good ideas that don't cost a fortune, type "more with less" into your browser and you'll find a Mennonite community full of great recipes and ideas.

Breads

Note: Why specify certain ingredients? Although unbleached white flour has had most of its nutrition stripped in milling, it has not been chemically treated to be white. Whole wheat flour, of course, has not been stripped of its nutrients. As for salt, use what you prefer. It's all right to insist on sea salt. Many people swear by it. All salt comes from salt mines that originated in the sea anyway. But olive oil is special. It has mono-unsaturated fatty acids (MUFAs) that actually feed your body. Canola oil is an acceptable second. We're feeding the body on limited resources, remember? Buy the best you can afford.

Biscuit Mix

6 cups unbleached white flour

2 cup whole wheat flour

1 1/3 cup powdered milk

2 teaspoons salt

6 tablespoons baking powder

1 cup canola or olive oil

Combine all dry ingredients thoroughly. Use a blender or food processor if you have one. Then blend in the oil and, again, mix thoroughly. Keep in a covered container in the refrigerator until needed. If larger containers are available, double the recipe.

Biscuits

Preheat oven to 425 degrees.

Combine in mixing bowl:

2 cups biscuit mix

1/2 cup water

Dough is soft and sticky. With floured hands, press dough onto floured board, pat out dough to 1/2 inch or taller. Use a light touch. Do not press down. You can pull apart dough into single biscuits, use a biscuit cutter, the top of a floured juice glass as a biscuit cutter, or you can cut biscuits into squares. They taste the same regardless of how you cut them.

Bake for 8-10 minutes on dry cookie sheet.

Yields 8 medium biscuits.

Cornbread

Preheat oven to 400 degrees.

Grease 9 inch square pan.

Combine in mixing bowl:

1 cup cornmeal

1 cup flour

1/4 cup sugar

4 teaspoons baking powder

3/4 teaspoon salt

Mix thoroughly, then add:

2 beaten eggs

1 cup water

1/4 cup oil

Mix together.

Place in greased 9 inch baking pan.

Bake for 20-25 minutes.

This is very good with honey, syrup, butter or milk.

Salt-Rising Bread

Ingredients:

- 1 cup milk
- 1/2 cup sifted cornmeal
- 4 cups milk
- 1 tablespoon sugar
- 14 to 16 cups sifted all-purpose flour
- 3/4 cup oil
- 1/2 cup sugar
- 1 tablespoon salt
- melted butter to brush tops of loaves

Preparation:

Scald 1 cup milk. Add sifted corn meal and cook until thick. Place in a quart jar with top and place in warm place to sour overnight. (Starter can be stored in the refrigerator for 1 to 2 weeks.) When bubbles form, it is ready to use. In a saucepan, combine 4 cups of milk and 1 tablespoon sugar and heat to scalding. Cool slightly and add to the cornmeal mixture in a large mixing bowl. Gradually stir 6 cups of flour. Set in warm place to rise until double (approximately 2 hours). Next, add oil, 1/2 cup sugar and salt. Mix well. Gradually add 6 cups of flour and work in. Put a generous dusting of flour on board and turn dough mixture onto board. Work in more flour and knead for about 20 minutes. Divide into four equal parts and put in greased and floured 9 1/2 x 5 1/2 x 2 3/4-inch loaf pans. Brush tops of loaves with oil and place in warm place to rise double (takes approximately 2 hours). Place in preheated 200° oven. Gradually turn heat up to 300°. Bake for 45 minutes. Take loaves out and brush tops with butter. Continue baking until done. Loaves will sound hollow when lightly tapped on bottom. Turn out on rack to cool. Total cooking will be approximately 1 hour to 1 hour and 15 minutes.

Sourdough

This is good for those who make a lot of bread and don't want to go to the store all the time to buy yeast. Why buy it when you can make sure you have a ready supply in the starter dough?

Sourdough bread is bread made without added yeast. By making a "starter" in which wild yeast can grow, the sourdough baker can raise bread naturally, as mankind did for thousands and thousands of years before a packet of yeast was an available convenience at the local market. Not all sourdough is sour-tasting; Amish Friendship Bread and other types of live-yeast breads are also sourdough.

To become a sourdough baker, all you need are some basic ingredients (flour, water, salt, and sugar), some basic tools (a non-metal mixing bowl, a non-metal spoon, an oven, and a baking sheet. This recipe is for the novice sourdough baker, but assumes that the reader is familiar with regular yeast-based baking. If you can make bread, you can make sourdough bread.

There are only a few simple steps to becoming a sourdough baker. First, you must create a starter: This is a bubbly batter that you keep in your fridge. The starter is mixed into a dough, and it causes the bread to rise. Bake and serve. Yum!

Creating Your Starter

The novel thing about sourdough baking is that it requires that you keep something alive in your fridge. Sourdough "starter" is a batter of flour and water, filled with living yeast and bacteria. The yeast and bacteria form a stable symbiotic relationship, and (as long as you keep the starter fed) it can live for years. It is a thriving colony of microorganisms. To make sourdough bread, you blend the starter with some flour and make dough. The yeast propagates, and leavens your bread. This is how you make your starter:

- **Select a container for your starter.** A wide-mouthed glass jar is best, such as a wide-mouthed mayonnaise or pickle jar. A small crock with a loose lid will also work. These can be bought in cheap sets for serving soup. You can also use a plastic container. Metallic containers can become reactive and can ruin your starter. For the same reason, **avoid using metal utensils to stir your starter**.
- **Blend a cup of warm water and a cup of flour, and pour it into the jar.** That's the whole recipe! You can use plain, unbleached bread flour, all-purpose or whole-wheat flour. If you want, you can add a little commercial yeast to a starter to "boost" it. Note that starter made with commercial yeast often produces bread with less distinctive sour flavor than the real thing.
- **Every 24 Hours, Feed the Starter.** You should keep the starter in a warm place. 70-80 degrees Fahrenheit is perfect. This allows the yeast already present in the flour (and in the air) to grow rapidly. Temperatures hotter than 100 degrees or so will kill it. You can take comfort from the fact that almost nothing else will do so. The way you feed the starter is to **(1)** throw away half of it and then **(2)** add a half-cup of

flour and a half-cup of water. Do this every 24 hours. Within three or four days, sometimes a week or more, you should start getting lots of bubbles throughout, and a pleasant beery smell. *When your starter develops a bubbly froth, it is done. You have succeeded.*

- **Refrigerate the Starter.** Keep the starter in your fridge, with a lid on it. Allow a little breathing space in the lid. If you're using a mayo or pickle jar, punch a hole in the lid with a nail so it can "breathe." It's alive, remember? Once the starter is chilled, it needs to be fed only once a week.

Care of the Starter

Aside from weekly feeding, the only other thing you need to worry about is a layer of watery liquid (yellow to brown) that contains alcohol. Don't drink it! The liquid builds up in your starter, and it's a normal part of the process. If your starter is looking dry, stir it back in. If your starter is wet enough, pour it off. Either way it won't matter.

Sourdough Baking Step One – Making a Sponge

- **Pour all your starter out of the jar and into a large non-metal bowl.** Then wash and dry your jar. Sterilize the jar with boiling water.
- **"Proof" your sponge.** Add 1 cup warm water and 1 cup flour to the bowl. Stir well. Set in warm place for several hours. You may proof your sponge overnight and use in the morning. The longer it sets out, the more sour the bread.
- **Use your sponge.** Your sponge will look bubbly with a white froth. It will smell a little sour.

Sourdough Baking Step Two – Baking Your Bread

- 2 cups of sponge (proofed starter)
- 3 cups of unbleached flour (approximately)
- 2 tablespoons of olive oil or softened margarine
- 4 teaspoons of sugar
- 2 teaspoons of salt

Put leftover sponge into the sterilized jar. Feed the starter with a half-cup each of flour and warm water and return it to the refrigerator for your next batch of bread.

Combine sugar, salt, and oil. Mix well. Knead in the flour a half a cup at a time until you have a smooth, elastic dough. You may not need all three cups of flour, or you may need more. A smooth elasticity is more important that the quantity of the flour.

Form into ball, cover loosely with a towel, and let rise in a warm place. Let rise until double in bulk. Sourdough often rises more slowly than other breads. When double, poke your finger into the dough. If it doesn't spring back, it's ready.

Punch the dough down, knead slightly and form into loaves (in loaf pans) or rounds (on a cookie sheet). Cover with your cloth or towel and let rise until double again.

Place risen dough in 350° oven. Bake 30-45 minutes. The bread is done when it sounds hollow when thumped. Put loaf onto a cooling rack or a towel and let cool. If you let your bread cool for at least an hour, it will cut better.

Tortillas

A few years ago someone wrote that too few possessed the talent for hand-making flatbreads. He claimed that in the near future, the only way to get them would be through stores and restaurants. Nonsense.

Mix together:

5 cups flour

2 teaspoons baking powder

¼ teaspoon salt

Add:

2 tablespoon oil

1 (or a little more) cup warm water

1. Knead a few minutes on floured surface until smooth and elastic. Lubricate top with oil, put back in bowl and let rest, covered for 10 minutes.
2. Divide into small balls the size of golf balls and proceed to roll out into size and thickness you prefer.
3. Cook on top of stove over medium heat using a cast iron grill or heavy skillet until top is slightly bubbly then turning on opposite side for a minute or two.
4. Keep stacked and warm inside a clean dish towel.

Fry Bread

This is another flatbread, this time made with yeast, but it's fried in a pan instead of baked on a griddle. Be careful of the amount of oil you use. You don't want to add a health problem to your limited budget. Use olive oil when you can afford it. Canola oil is a good second.

4 cups flour
2 tbsp. baking powder
1 tsp. salt
1/2 cup cooking oil
1 cup warm water

Mix flour, baking powder and salt. Gradually add in the shortening and water. Add only enough water to make dough stick together. Knead dough until smooth, make into fist-sized balls. Cover them with a towel for 10 minutes then pat them out into circles about the size of a pancake. Fry in hot cooking oil in cast iron skillet until brown on both sides. Serve with jam. Yummy!

French Bread

French bread is a delicious limited-resource bread. It's a yeast bread that has no milk in the ingredients, so it's also good for those who are lactose intolerant.

1 1/4 cups warm water
1 (1/4-ounce) package active dry yeast *or* 2 1/2 teaspoons active dry yeast
1 tablespoon granulated sugar
1 tablespoon oil

1 1/2 teaspoons salt
3 1/2 cups flour
1 large egg, beaten
1 tablespoon sesame seeds (optional)

1. Pour warm water (105° to 115°F) into a large bowl; sprinkle yeast over top. Stir in sugar, shortening and salt. Add flour, 1/2 cup at a time, until mixture forms a soft dough. Knead until smooth, about 5 minutes; leave covered with a tea towel in a warm place; allow to rise for at least 60 minutes or until doubled in bulk.
2. Preheat oven to 350°F. Meanwhile generously grease a 9 x 5 x 3-inch loaf pan; punch down to press out air; place in pan. Allow to rise for about 60 minutes or until doubled in bulk.
3. Slash the top diagonally in two or three places, brush with egg, sprinkle with sesame seeds.
4. Bake for 30 minutes or until golden brown. Bread will make a hollow sound when tapped.

Makes 1 loaf.

Tip: French bread can also be baked on a flat sheet and shaped by hand. A one-pound loaf, rolled into a long shape and slashed diagonally along its length, is called a baguette, French for 'rod.'

Wheat Bread

You can use all whole wheat flour, if you wish, but that makes a very heavy bread. I lighten it with some unbleached white flour.

Mix together:

2 cups unbleached white flour

1 package yeast

In small saucepan combine, and heat until warm (115' to 120'):

1 ¾ cups water

1/3 cup brown sugar

3 tablespoons oil

Add to dry mixture. Mix thoroughly.

Stir in:

2 cups whole wheat flour

Put 1 cup unbleached white flour onto bread board. Spread out.

Dump dough onto pile of white flour and knead in. Knead 8 to 10 minutes.

You may need to add more flour, but only add a little at a time after you've kneaded in the 1 cup of unbleached white flour.

Shape into ball. Place in lightly greased bowl, turning once.

Cover with damp towel. Let rise in warm place until double, about 1 ½ hours.

Punch down. Dump onto lightly floured surface. Divide in half and let rest 10 minutes.

Form into loaves. Place in 2 greased loaf pans.

Put in 250' oven for 40-50 minutes.

Hot Dinner Rolls

These are refrigerator rolls, so those of you with limited time can still treat your guests to the treat of home-made, piping hot dinner rolls. Isn't life great?

Day before: mix together:

1 ½ cups flour

1 package yeast

In saucepan, warm (115' to 120'):

1 ¼ cups milk

¼ cup sugar

¼ cup oil

1 teaspoon salt

Add to dry mixture.

Add 1 egg.

Mix thoroughly.

A little at a time, spoon in and mix together 2 cups flour. This will be a softer dough than the bread dough.

Form into ball. Place into greased bowl, turning once. Put in refrigerator until 2 hours before dinner the next day.

Next day: Form into desires shapes, cover with cloth, let rise until double (about 1 to 1 ½ hours), bake at 350' 10-12 minutes.

Cereals

Cereals are grains that have been processed. Processed cereals can be very expensive. Furthermore, they usually have far too much sugar added than is healthy. If you can afford these sweetened treats, great. But if your dollars are tight, try some of these recipes.

Unsweetened Cereal (packaged) and Milk

This is my favorite cereal. I use corn flakes. I've also used crisp rice. But any unsweetened cereal will work.

1 cup unsweetened, packaged cereal

¼ cup raisins

¼ cup roasted, unsalted sunflower seeds

1 cup milk.

Put everything in a bowl, eat with a spoon and know that you've fed your body with good nutrition.

1 serving.

Cooked Rice Cereal

(4 servings)

- 1 ½ cups white rice—uncooked
- 2 cups lowfat milk (or soy milk—vanilla soy milk works great)
- ¼ cup sugar
- 1 ½ teaspoons of ground cinnamon

Prepare the rice according to the directions on the package.
Combine warm cooked rice, milk, sugar, and cinnamon. Stir and serve. That's all there is to it.

Great as a dry snack or with milk for breakfast. Stores well in sealed plastic container for a week.

Honey Maple Grapenuts

(This recipe yields 12 servings)

- 3 cups whole wheat or graham flour
- 1/2 cup barley flour or rye flour
- 1/3 cup tapioca flour or oat flour
- 1/3 cup toasted wheat germ
- 1/2 cup dry milk powder
- 1/2 cup brown sugar
- 1/2 teaspoon salt
- 2 teaspoons baking soda
- 2 teaspoons maple flavoring
- 1/4 cup warmed honey or maple syrup
- 1/2 cup buttermilk
- 1-2 teaspoons cinnamon and nutmeg (optional)

Preheat oven to 325 degrees.

Sift the dry ingredients -- blend thoroughly.

Beat the liquid ingredients together.

Stir wet ingredients into dry ingredients.

If resulting mixture is watery work in a little additional flour.

Spread on 2 or 3 baking sheets and bake for 10-15 minutes. Stir to break up granules and bake 10 minutes longer or until golden brown.

Cool and store in air-tight container.

Makes about 2 pounds or roughly two boxes of cereal.

Apple Granola

Mix together:

4 cups old-fashioned rolled oats

½ cup coconut

1 cup nuts, finely chopped

½ cup sesame seed

1 teaspoon cinnamon

In another bowl combine:

1/2 cup honey

1/3 cup oil

1/2 teaspoon vanilla

Add to dry ingredients and mix thoroughly.

Spread out on greased baking sheet.

Bake 20-25 minutes at 350', stirring occasionally

Add 8 ounces finely cut dried apples

Store in tightly covered container in refrigerator.

Dry Old-Fashioned Oats

Pour ¼ cup of old fashioned oatmeal (uncooked) into a bowl. Top with ¼ - ½ cup of yogurt. Then top with chopped apples and raisins. Mix together. Delicious!

You can vary the toppings to your liking, such as using roasted unsalted sunflower seeds or grapes in addition to apples and raisins.

To keep this recipe frugal, buy the large 4.5 pound bag of raisins and the 32 oz. container of yogurt.

Cooked Oatmeal Variations

Cook oatmeal as instructed.

Instead of just adding milk and sugar, you can also try:

Butter

Brown sugar

Maple syrup, flavoring

Other flavored syrups, such as blueberry or strawberry

Cinnamon or cinnamon sugar

Diced apples, bananas, peaches, pears, strawberries

Raisins or other dried fruit

Sliced almonds, chopped pecans or other roasted, unsalted nuts

Cooked Breakfasts

Shirred, or Baked Eggs

You can bake eggs nestled in other foods such as rice, vegetables or sauces. These foods should be heated before the eggs are added for faster and more even cooking. Make indentations in the heated food with the back of a spoon, about 2-inch diameter

For individual servings of baked eggs, use baking dishes (ramekins, custard cups, individual soufflé dishes, or small oval bakers) that just fit the eggs plus the flavoring, food, or liquid. If baking the eggs in other solid foods or in liquids, preheat them before adding the eggs for faster and more even cooking.

- Preheat oven to 325° F.
- For each serving, lightly butter an individual oven-proof baking dish or ramekin.
- Break one or two eggs into each dish. Season with salt and pepper. Spoon 1 tablespoon milk or cream over eggs (skim milk, low-fat milk, half and half, or light cream may be substituted). Spooning a liquid over the eggs can help prevent drying out. Bake in preheated oven approximately 12 to 14 minutes, depending on number of servings being baked. Check the eggs after about 10 minutes baking time. When done, the whites should be completely set and the yolks beginning to thicken but not hard.

Serve Immediately.

Approximate Time for Boiled Eggs

Egg Size	Degree of Doneness	Time Required
Medium	Soft-cooked yolk	3 minutes
	Medium-cooked yolk	5 minutes
	Hard-cooked yolk	12 minutes
Large	Soft-cooked yolk	4 to 5 minutes
	Medium-cooked yolk	6 minutes
	Hard-cooked yolk	17 minutes
Extra Large	Soft-cooked yolk	5 minutes
	Medium-cooked yolk	7 to 8 minutes
	Hard-cooked yolk	19 minutes

Creamy Eggs Over Biscuits

Hard boil 6 eggs. Set aside.

Melt in saucepan:

2 tablespoons butter

Add:

2 tablespoons flour until it forms into a ball.

Slowly add:

2 cups milk, stirring continuously until the sauce comes to a boil

Salt and pepper to taste.

Chop the eggs into the sauce. Reheat, stir together until eggs are heated.

For variations, you may also add green peppers, red peppers, mushrooms, onions, chopped tomatoes.

You may garnish with chives or green onions or sprinkle cheese on top.

Omelets

I've never mastered the art of letting the scrambled egg mixture flow under the cooked egg. This is the way I do omelets, and they're delicious!

Set aside:

Grated cheese.

Chopped onion, chopped green and red peppers, jalapenos, mushrooms, chopped tomatoes, or anything else you may want to put on your omelets.

Place 2 eggs into small bowl and beat with fork.

Put egg mixture into moderately hot oil. Too hot and the eggs will burn before they're done, too cool and they'll take forever to cook.

Add toppings beginning with raw ones first, such as the onions or peppers.

Add a handful of cheese as the last ingredient.

When the edges begin to darken a little, your cheese should also be melting nicely. Fold over in half with pancake turner, and then turn over completely. This allows any uncooked egg to spill out and get done.

Serve with toast or biscuits. Delicious!

1 serving

Huevos Rancheros

Eating cheap foods? Tired of beans? This is the best way to use those leftover beans!

Have ready:

Hot beans

Tortillas

Grated cheese

Salsa

Jalapeno peppers

Fry a couple of eggs. Put them on a tortilla that has been spread with mashed beans. Add salsa to taste. Cover with a handful of grated cheese. Salt, pepper and jalapenos to taste.

Breakfast Burritos

This is yet another way to use up leftovers. Chop cooked vegetables and cooked potatoes and set aside. Also have ready chopped onions, green and red peppers, mushrooms, grated cheese. Can you tell I live in the Southwest?

Scramble eggs.

Put a spoonful of scrambled eggs onto a tortilla.

Add whatever vegetables you like.

Wrap in a tortilla and serve.

Salsa or hot sauce to taste.

Pancakes

Mix together:

2 cups flour

2 tablespoons sugar

3 teaspoons baking powder

1/3 cup dry milk powder

Add:

2 beaten eggs

2 tablespoons oil

2 cups water (approximately)

Pour onto lightly greased griddle or pan. When bubbles form on top, turn. Bake until lightly browned on bottom. Adjust heat if necessary.

Pancake Variations:

- Add 1 finely chopped apple to mix.
- Make half the flour whole wheat or buckwheat.
- Use honey instead of sugar.
- While bottom of pancake is baking, add a few blueberries before turning.
- Substitute buttermilk or sour milk for the milk, then add ½ teaspoon to the mix, and reduce baking powder to 1 tablespoon.

Soups and Sandwiches

Tip: Save vegetable water in refrigerator for soups.

Soups are real dollar-stretchers. They are also excellent ways to use up leftovers. When my husband got paid weekly, our Friday meal was usually soup, whatever we had leftover. We called the soup Refrigerator. I would have the soup ready for when he got home, and we would go shopping for groceries afterwards. Be judicious. Not everything goes well in soup. Some leftovers are better as dog food.

Potato Soup with Green Onions

Boil 2-3 potatoes, save water, or use leftover potatoes. You have followed the tip and save your vegetable water, right?

Add garlic to taste.

Add salt/pepper to taste.

Make a paste of ¼ cup flour to 1 cup water and add to soup broth.

Cook until soup thickens.

Add 2 cups milk, heat until warm. Bring to just bubbly then remove from heat.

Top with 2 tablespoons butter and garnish each bowl with freshly chopped chives or green onions.

My husband's mother added green beans and dumplings to her potato soup.

Grandma's Butter Dumplings

Mix together:

1 cup flour

$\frac{1}{2}$ teaspoon baking powder

1 teaspoon salt (yes, I know this makes them kind of salty, but you don't need crackers)

Add:

1 beaten egg

4 tablespoons butter

Dough should be stiff. Some of it may also be in crumbles. Add the crumbles to the soup first. They help thicken the broth.

Drop teaspoons of dough into bubbling broth.

Cook until dumplings are done.

Now you can add milk and reheat. For thicker soups, add less milk.

Chili

Mix together:

1 cup flour

½ teaspoon baking powder

1 teaspoon salt (yes, I know this makes them kind of salty, but you don't need crackers)

Add:

1 beaten egg

4 tablespoons butter

Dough should be stiff. Some of it may also be in crumbles. Add the crumbles to the soup first. They help thicken the broth.

Drop teaspoons of dough into bubbling broth.

Cook until dumplings are done.

Now you can add milk and reheat. For thicker soups, add less milk.

Add all the rest of the ingredients and bring to a simmer. You may simmer this all day if you like. Just keep adding water for consistency. This is one dish that's better later than earlier.

Serve with grated cheese and chopped onions as garnishes.

Bean Soup Variations

Add cooked rice to leftover beans and its broth.

Add vegetables and beef broth to make bean vegetable soup.

Add macaroni and tomatoes with oregano and basil for an Italian flavor.

Quick-Cook Beans

You've always heard to soak your beans overnight. True. But your company is coming tonight, and all you have is beans. What do you do?

Put rinsed beans in a pot. Cover with water. Bring to rapid boil.

Remove from heat. Let stand for 1 hour. Cook beans as desired.

Can you really serve company beans? Of course you can. If they're quality people, they came to see you, not to see what you have for dinner.

Perfect Pea Soup

1 package of split peas.
Note: some packages have a flavor packet included, delicious!
9 cups water
1 medium onion, chopped fine (optional)
1 tablespoon minced garlic
2 carrots, grated or diced
1 cooked ham slice, diced
4 tablespoons butter or margerine
1-2 teaspoons salt (to taste)
1/4 to 1/2 teaspoon pepper
1/2 cup dry milk mixed with 1 cup water,
stirred until all lumps gone

Put split peas, water, onion, garlic, carots, ham and water in large pot. Bring to rapid boil. Reduce heat to simmer. Simmer, stirring occasionally for 1-2 hours, until stirred soup is thick and the peas no longer lumpy. Add butter or margerine, salt, pepper, seasoning packet, if incuded, add mixed milk. May add more milk to taste.

Note: if you're lactose intolerant you may leave out the milk and it will taste just fine.
Serve hot with crackers, croutons, biscuits or freshly-baked bread. It's also good served cold garnished with chopped chives or green onions.

Hearty Lentil Stew

- 7 medium potatoes, chopped (can substitute cooked rice for the potatoes)
- 2 cans of diced tomatoes, or substitute 1 can of Rotel tomatoes for 1 can of diced tomatoes if you like your stew spicy
- 1 large onion, chopped
- 2 cloves garlic, minced
- 1 pound Polish sausage, sliced (nice, but another meat, if you have it, will also work)
- 1 (16 ounce) package lentils
- salt and pepper to taste

1. Place the potatoes, tomatoes, onion, garlic, and sausage in a large pot with enough water to cover. Bring to a boil, and cook 15 minutes.
2. Stir lentils into the pot. Add more water if necessary to just cover all ingredients. Season with salt and pepper. Bring to a boil. Reduce heat to medium-low, and continue cooking 20 minutes, stirring occasionally, until lentils are tender.

Green Chili Soup

Leftover pork chops? Leftover pork roast? Can't afford either, but love pork? This recipe uses the meat from 2 pork chops.

Boil 2 pork loin chops until meat is falling off bone.

Remove bone. Cut meat into ½ inch cubes.

Add: 1 medium onion

        ¼ cup garlic, minced

        ¼ cup cilantro

        1 tablespoon cumin

        1 large can chopped green chilies

        1 can Rotel Tomatoes with peppers

        1 ½ teaspoons garlic salt

Simmer until done, which means any time after all the ingredients are brought to a simmer. This is one of those dishes that are better when served later.

Serve with chopped chives or green onions and shredded cheese as garnishes.

Egg & Cheese Sandwiches

There are several ways to make egg and cheese sandwiches.

1. You can scramble the eggs first.
2. You can toast the bread, or not.
3. You can spread mayonnaise, mustard or butter on your bread.
4. You can put the cheese inside the scramble egg or serve it in slices.
5. You can fry the egg, instead of scrambling it, with the yolk pierced so it forms an egg patty.
6. You can use a variety of breads, rye, whole wheat, sourdough. All make excellent egg sandwiches.
7. Add sliced tomatoes, lettuce, an onion slice, or sprouts to your sandwich. Yummm!

Grilled Cheese Sandwiches

Butter any kind of bread on one side, all slices.

Place bread slices in moderate skillet, butter side down. Butter burns easily, so don't get your skillet too hot.

Add slice of cheese.

Add second slice of bread, butter side up.

When bottom slice is browned, turn and brown other side.

Serve hot with sliced tomatoes or other fresh fruit or vegetables.

Chicken Quesadillas

Have a microwave? This is an easy, fun, delicious and nutritious—and quick!—meal.

2 tortillas per quesadilla.

Place 1 tortilla on plate

Add chopped chicken, and any or all of the following:

- Mushrooms
- Chopped onion
- Chopped green chilies
- Chopped green or red pepper
- Chopped tomato
- Sliced black olives

Cover with grated cheese.

Top with another tortilla.

Microwave for 1 minute, or less, depending on the microwave.

With pizza cutter, cut into wedges.

Serve with dollops of salsa, sour cream and/or guacamole.

Dinners

I used to work for an outfitter as a camp cook. I can cook over an open campfire, a wood stove, a propane stove, a natural gas stove, a Coleman stove, or at home with my electric stove. The only place I have trouble cooking is in someone else's kitchen. As long as the kitchen is mine, even if it's in a cook tent, I can cook.

But I'm not a gourmet chef. I'm a plain, home style cook who can take whatever is on hand and make a meal out of it. I have cooked squirrel, rabbit, raccoon, rock chuck (marmot or ground hog), quail, grouse, pheasant, deer, elk, bear, and even porcupine.

Once while working for the outfitter, one of our guests shot a grouse. He brought back the dead bird and asked if I could cook it for him. Of course I could. That evening, in the cook tent, I fixed steaks and his grouse. He was delighted.

These recipes contain more common foods, and very little meat. Unless you can hunt for meat, or you can afford to buy it, cheap entrees use meat sparingly. That doesn't mean you can't eat well, of course. Each recipe is a complete protein. But each recipe is also high in carbohydrates and calories. So, once again, be judicious. Only you know the nutritional needs of your family.

Macaroni and Cheese

All right, buy a box and have fun. But if you just went to the food bank and they gave you a package of macaroni noodles, and you've never made scratch macaroni and cheese before, here's one recipe. First of all, I use real cheese, not a cheese spread or a soft processed cheese. This recipe uses a good hard cheese. But, if someone gave you a brick of American cheese, you can substitute that. Use what you have and be grateful for it; don't wish for what you don't have. That's the key to being happy right where you are.

Cook macaroni per instructions. If water is a luxury where you live, you may save the water back for soups and for the cheese sauce:

In saucepan over medium to low heat, melt 4 tablespoons butter.

Add ½ cup flour and stir until it forms a ball.

Add 1 cup of milk, reconstituted dry milk, canned milk, or water very slowly. Stir out any lumps.

Add 1 cup grated cheese, again very slowly. You want the cheese to melt in the sauce. If you need to add liquid, you may add either milk or water.

Put macaroni in lightly greased baking dish.

Pour sauce over macaroni and stir together.

Sprinkle grated cheese over top.

Place in 350' oven.

Bake for ½ hour, or until lightly browned on top.

Scalloped Potatoes with Cheese

You can fix scalloped potatoes without cheese, and by using milk it will be a complete protein. But scalloped potatoes *with* cheese is best. But sometimes there's just no cheese. I know. I've been there.

5-8 potatoes, or more, depending on the army you need to feed.

Scrub and peel potatoes. (I don't peel mine. The peel adds nutrition.)

Slice thinly and arrange one layer in a greased or buttered baking dish.

Sprinkle flour over potatoes.

Add salt and pepper.

Sprinkle a layer of grated cheese over the floured and seasoned potatoes.

Repeat with at least one more layer of seasoned and floured potatoes.

Top with one layer of grated cheese.

Add milk (reconstituted dry milk is best because you can add a little more water to stretch the milk) to a little over half full.

Put in 350' oven for 1 hour.

If top cheese starts burning before hour is up, put some aluminum foil over it. If you used more than two layers, you may need to adjust your oven time. If a fork goes in easily and it's bubbling nicely, your dish is done.

Potatoes with Bacon or Sausage Gravy

Remember what makes up a complete protein? Do we need meat? No, but we do need a complete protein, which means potatoes and cream gravy is a complete protein. Yea!

With sausage gravy, use the drippings of one or two crumbled sausage patties.

Leave the sausage in the pan.

Add enough flour to ball up the grease.

Add reconstituted dry milk or canned milk (Please! You don't want to use up your good drinking milk for this!) a little at a time, stirring constantly, until the gravy is bubbling and you have achieved the desired consistency.

For bacon gravy, I always pre-cut the bacon into tiny pieces and cook the small pieces. Fry until very crisp.

Add enough flour to ball up the grease.

Add reconstituted milk a little at a time, stirring constantly, until the gravy is bubbling and you have achieved the desired consistency.

Salt and pepper to taste.

Serve either one over cooked potatoes.

Delicious!

Cheesy Rice and Broccoli

I actually "invented" this recipe before I found that someone else already had. Our family loves it.

Boil rice according to directions.

Cook broccoli according to directions; steaming is best and retains more food value. Use the leftover water to make your cheese sauce.

In saucepan melt 2 tablespoons of butter.

Add enough flour to make the butter ball up.

Add about 1 cup of reconstituted dry milk using your broccoli water.

Add 1 cup grated cheese a little at a time until all cheese melts. Your gravy should be thick.

Add broccoli.

Add broccoli and cheese to rice. Stir and serve, or stir and bake with a layer of grated cheese on top in 350' oven for ½ hour.

Lasagna

Here is another way to use ground turkey, except this time, use turkey sausage. No need to buy expensive Italian sausage.

1 pound ground turkey sausage

Brown sausage slowly, spooning off any fat.

Add and bring to simmer:

- 1 tablespoon minced garlic
- 1 tablespoon basil
- 1 tablespoon oregano
- 1 pound can tomatoes, chopped.
- 1 small can tomato paste
- 1 cup water

Simmer 15 minutes, stirring often.

Cook lasagna noodles as directed.

Make cheese filling by combining:

- 3 cups cottage cheese
- ½ cup grated Parmesan or Romano cheese
- 2 tablespoons parsley flakes
- 1 teaspoon salt
- ½ teaspoon pepper

Layer half the cooked noodles in 13 x 9 x 2 inch pan.

Spoon half the cottage cheese filling over the noodles.

Add one layer of thinly sliced mozzarella cheese.

Add half the meat sauce. Repeat.

Bake at 375' for 30 minutes. Mmmm!

Black Beans and Yellow Rice

Spicy Black Beans

- 2 cups (about 1 pound) dried black beans, picked over, soaked overnight
- 3 tablespoons extra-virgin olive oil
- 1/2 medium onion, diced
- 1 jalapeno pepper, chopped (may leave this out if you don't like spicy foods)
- 2 cloves garlic, chopped
- 1 bay leaf
- Salt
- Black pepper

In a large pot, soak beans overnight covered in water by 2 inches. Drain and set aside.

In the same pot, heat the olive oil. Add the onion, jalapeno pepper, garlic, and bay leaf and cook until the vegetables begin to soften, about 5 minutes. Add the beans and cover with water by about 1-inch. Bring to a boil, reduce the heat, cover, and simmer for 1 to 1 1/2 hours, or until the beans are tender. Remove the bay leaf and discard. Taste the beans and season with salt and pepper.

Yellow Rice:

- 2 cups rice
- 4 cups water
- 2 cloves garlic, smashed
- 1 tablespoon turmeric
- 1 teaspoon salt
- 1 bay leaf

Put all the ingredients into a heavy-bottomed pot, stir well, and bring to a boil over medium-high heat. Reduce the heat to a simmer, cover, and cook over low heat until the rice has absorbed the water, about 15 to 20 minutes, 40 minutes if you use brown rice. Remove from the heat and let sit, covered, for 5 minutes. Discard the bay leaf, fluff with a fork, and serve alongside the beans.

Yummy!

Beans and Tortillas

Anasazi beans are best. Cook according to directions. Have chopped tomatoes, grated cheese, chopped onions, and any other sides (such as sour cream and guacamole) ready. Serve with tortillas. Very basic, but very good!

Desserts

I'm not going to spend any time on desserts. We all know what we love to eat, and I'm not going to challenge that. But here are a couple of old recipes that add nutrition along with the calories.

Bread Pudding

If you go to the food bank, the chances are you get more bread than you can use. And because money is so tight, you hate to throw anything away, even when it's free. One answer is to keep your bread in the refrigerator or freezer. It will last longer. But the next suggestion tastes better. Make bread pudding.

You'll need:

- Old, non-moldy bread, crumbled. If there's a spot or two of mold, you can pinch off the moldy parts and still use the good bread. But if you've found one spot of mold, check each slice thoroughly.
- A large, lightly greased, baking dish.
- 1 egg per cup of bread
- 1 cup of reconstituted dry or canned milk per cup of bread
- ¼ cup of brown sugar per cup of bread
- ¼ cup of raisins per 2 cups of bread
- ¼ teaspoon vanilla per cup of bread
- ¼ teaspoon cinnamon per cup of bread

Assemble all ingredients in large mixing bowl.

Pour into large, lightly greased, baking dish.

Place baking dish inside a larger dish with 1" of water.

Bake at 350' for about an hour, more or less, depending on how much you made, until knife inserted in the middle comes out clean.

Rice Pudding

Preheat oven to 275'

Butter baking dish.

Combine in mixing bowl:

- 4 cups milk, scalded (that means heated until a skin forms on top of the milk, just before boiling. Remove the skin before using.)
- 1/3 cup rice
- 1/3 cup sugar
- 1/4 teaspoon salt
- Dash of nutmeg, cinnamon or finely grated orange peel.

Bake 2 to 2 ½ hours until rice is tender and milk is creamy, stirring occasionally during first hour of baking time. Rice (optional) can be added during last half hour of baking time.

Put in refrigerator to cool. Pudding will thicken in the refrigerator.

Chapter 2

Entertainment

While attending Denver Seminary I had a professor who hated all electronic amusement, but especially television and movies. His aversion to media enjoyment spilled even into his assignments. We were required to "fast" for a week from TV, and to write a paper on our responses. He took his position against TV to the extreme, even buying a universal remote and turning off the TVs in stores. His logic was that TV replaced thinking. It gave the watcher no chance for an intelligent exchange of thought. It provided a false sense of what is acceptable and not acceptable. In the TV world attitudes are defined by cartoon characters. Morality is defined by dysfunctional sitcom families. TV promotes violence, selfishness, and materialism to the point of overspending, one reason we are in a financial mess. In addition, it replaces our ability to entertain ourselves, which our society used to do.

Whether or not I accept his point of view, it is true that we have become so used to others entertaining us too many of us no longer know how to entertain ourselves. Suppose we found creative ways to entertain ourselves, such as: crafting gifts, wood carving, writing a skit for the family or for church and producing it, learning to play an instrument, picking up needle crafts such as knitting or crocheting, sewing, mending. We have too much to do, more time to waste, and no time to do anything constructive. Let's learn to play with purpose.

Family Entertainment

Some families spend their time taking their children from one event to another: soccer, ballet, martial arts, to name a fraction of children's activities, all of which cost the family plenty. If you recently lost your job, however, these become luxuries, not the necessities you imagined at first.

Other families, people who never could afford the local football league, work so many hours they are never home either. Maybe it's time to slow down and take advantage of being home together and learn to play as a family. You can find a number of ideas on family activities by querying on the internet with the words "family time fun." A whole string of affordable family activity websites will pop up. Let me suggest a few free ideas besides board games and card games, although those can be fun too.

Storytelling, for example, is nearly a lost art form. But you can develop it by beginning a story, then having each one in the family add a part to the story. Be forewarned: children have wild imaginations. Your story might get extremely crazy, but it will also be extraordinary fun.

Paper crafts are popular with children. You could use the library as a resource for origami and other paper crafts. Paper crafts can be used to celebrate a number of holidays, such as Valentine's Day, 4th Of July, Thanksgiving and Christmas.

On May Day, which is not celebrated anymore because the Communists took it over, we used to make paper baskets and fill them with flowers, then give them to the elderly and shut-ins in our neighborhood. In those days we knew our neighbors. We knew who had just lost a dog, who needed transportation to and from work or day care because their car had just broken down.

A friend of mine told a story about his father who went to the garage to find his car gone. He did not call the police. When his son asked about it, he said, "Well, I think it was just a neighbor who needed it for a while. He'll bring it back."

The neighbor had indeed taken his car because of a family emergency, and hadn't had time to leave a note. The car was back by evening. No police needed to become involved. We also used to leave our doors unlocked during that time in American history, but those days are over. Now, in addition to being unable to entertain ourselves, we imprison ourselves in our homes and never even meet our neighbors.

Dining IN with Friends

But some things need to change, and getting to know our neighbors is one of them. It's a kind of insurance. We know who we like, have a better idea of who to trust, and know who we prefer to avoid.

One way to solve an entertainment problem and to solve the problem of how to afford eating out is to dine with friends. Our church promoted a couples dining club called Tables of Eight. After a while it occurred to the club that most people did not have tables that seated eight. Furthermore, many singles would have loved to join, but they understood it was for couples. So we developed Tables of Six and included singles, which proved to be much more popular.

You don't need to belong to a church to start a dining-out club. You only need friends. Neither do you need a table, especially if yours only seats four. You can entertain in your living room or kitchen or allow people run of the whole house. It's your event, make it as fancy or as plain as you like. You can include a babysitter, or take turns providing that service, just so you know that the idea is a night out, away from work and other responsibilities, like rearing children.

Neither do you need to provide entertainment. The idea of having a dining-out club is to get to know each other better, and that means learning to talk to each other.

Skits and Plays

Now, why would I include skits and plays as a form of entertainment? Who wants a stupid script, and who would ever watch a bunch of amateurs performing?

The idea is cheap entertainment, remember? Something better than TV. Or maybe just an alternative to watching something canned for the mindless. I never said you were either a professional actor or a scriptwriter. This is a chance to think beyond your normal boundaries and experience more of life despite your circumstances.

Just so you know, I'm not a professional scriptwriter. The only scripts I have written were telemarketing scripts, skits for various church groups or organizations, or short plays for special groups.

So you probably know more than I do. Run with it. I won't stand in your way. But neither will I accept criticism from a professional scriptwriter. This isn't meant to be professional. This is meant to be fun.

The idea of a script is to know what needs to be said or done next. It doesn't offer tips on how to act unless it's part of the script, such as George and Martha. In that script, the only words said are "George" and "Martha." It starts out as if George is coming home from work. He calls out, "Martha." She responds with a welcoming, "George." The skit continues through an argument and ends with them making up afterwards.

Most skits are simple. Actual plays can become much more complicated, but the design is the same. Props can be practically non-existent, such as in the three-act play by Thornton Wilder, "Our Town," or as intricate as a movie set. You can go to your local library for instructions on how to write a script, or even to find a script to play with. Practice writing a skit, then produce it. It's much more fun, and certainly more interactive than television.

Music

Music is as old as humanity. We are born to it. True, some of us are tone deaf, but most of us can sing along with the radio. But music also needs to be interactive. I mourn the loss of choirs, where amateur voices got together to praise God and aid worship. Now we watch others do our music for us, and sort of sing along at appropriate times. Then we clap and give them praise. It feels good to clap. It feels good to receive praise. But I must ask the question, to whom are we giving praise?

I sang in two choirs, one at church, and another that celebrated my own heritage. Both were volunteer choirs made up, primarily, of amateur voices. We loved to sing.

Music, however, can be more than singing. When we send our children to school to learn to play in band, we are adding music to our community. We could, if this is something we have always wanted to do, learn to play our child's instrument. Or we could take up a simple instrument ourselves. Recently I picked up an Irish whistle, which is kind of like a recorder. It's not hard to play, compared to a flute or clarinet, but I am having trouble regulating the air flow, just as if I were playing a clarinet. With practice I'll get better. That's the joy of it, just playing. As long as I am less critical, I can have more fun.

Simple instruments include autoharps, where you press a bar with the chord labeled, and just strum. Guitars can be easy also, if all you need are chords to back up your voice. With a few chords, you can just strum, and sing your heart out. Or you could get fancy and really learn to play the guitar, which is not easy, but very rewarding as you gain mastery.

My point is, be a part of your music, not just a spectator. We are a nation of spectators. Life happens to us. Even when we vote, we watch others take charge of our lives. We listen, sometimes sing along, but don't own the music around us, or the political climate, or the preached word, or someone else's interpretation of the Bible. We watch life unfold as if it's television. We work to pay on credit cards that make someone else rich, but we don't have to. We could pay off our bills. We could learn to identify our own theology, and explore the reasons we believe as we do. We could write letters to our political leaders, over and over again until we're heard. It's not too late to snatch back ownership.

Owning music is a fun way to start.

Chapter 3

Healthy Altitudes

Beech Aircraft voted to strike. There were no food stamps or assistance for strikers. To supplement our non-existent income, my husband found part-time work in a gas station making $35 a week (this was a while ago). So when he wasn't walking with the rest of the strikers, he was working. I was a stay-at-home mom, which has always been my favorite profession. We were a young family, me barely into my twenties with two babies under three.

In those days rent was $65 a month and utilities about $35. It was *back in the day*. My husband's first two weeks' income went for the rent. The third went for utilities. That's nearly a month without buying groceries, folks. We had a kitchen full of groceries when the strike started. Well, since Beech Aircraft paid weekly, we had a week's supply of groceries in the house plus a few other items.

The first week wasn't so bad. I saved back all the groceries I could and began to skip breakfast so that the babies could eat and so that my husband would still get supper. The next week we cooked our last of the meat, a pork roast that I made last all week. We ate pork roast two days, pork stew the next three days, and by using the drippings in the roasting pan, we ate pork gravy over potatoes the sixth day… This was week two. I quit eating lunch.

The third week I used up the rest of the flour, cornmeal, powdered milk, canned milk, and all but one can of sweet potatoes, although the kids still had breakfast cereal left. I wouldn't touch it. Neither would I touch any other food item until supper when I made a meal for my husband and ate a little so that he wouldn't need to worry about that too. But by the end of the third week, I was starving. We still had the can of sweet potatoes. I had no idea what we would have for supper that evening.

I warmed up the sweet potatoes for the kids for lunch. It wasn't a complete protein. Remember in the first chapter where I outline what is needed for a complete protein? They ate the way babies do, eating a bit and playing with the rest. When they began to play with the food, I took it away and finished it off myself, literally licking their plates clean.

After naps the kids began crying because they were hungry. I became incensed and slapped them both. "I'm hungry too," I yelled at them.

Then I began to sob, ashamed that I had hit my babies for crying. Although I had been praying throughout this whole experience, I prayed again, deeper this time. I asked God why this was happening to us. Did I receive a reply? I think so. I understood that we weren't the only ones going through this time, and that the skills I learned during this time would help us through others, which led me to believe that if there would be other times, and that we had a future. We would survive this and other desperate times. We did. And we have.

Still, that was probably one of the lowest points in my life. When my husband came home, we had no supper. I asked him how much money he had, and he told me we had a dime. So we took our last coin, went downtown, and fed it into the parking meter. That afternoon I got a job as a waitress working afternoons and nights. I knew I could count on two things: I would get a free meal working as a waitress (they paid seventy-five cents an hour in those days), and by my break at eight o'clock, I would have enough tip money for my husband to buy some supper for himself and the babies.

Why relate this story under the heading of Healthy Altitudes? No matter what your circumstances, if you begin now to hold your head at a healthy altitude, your attitude will shift along with it. I want to let you know that unhealthy ways of thinking creep in when we are desperate, but it isn't the end of the world when they do.

By the way, I never lost a pound during that month. Our bodies hold onto every calorie when stressed, just for such times as these. I'm fat now (in my sixties), because we have had a number of hungry times, and when dieting, my body goes into survival mode and refuses to lose weight. So when dieting I need to do several things, get enough rest, avoid stress and *eat*. Odd, isn't it?

Keep the Job You Have

In this economy, the world seems to turn upside down. I have a Master's degree, but in my last job I worked at a boys' group home which paid poorly compared to the earnings I should have expected with my degree. I loved my work, which was fortunate. But once during a recent period of unemployment I worked as a temporary data entry clerk at Enstrom's Almond Toffee through their Christmas rush. Enstrom's does ninety percent of their business during the six-week Christmas season. Since they offered overtime, I worked as many hours as they would allow, and saved enough for two month's rent. After Christmas was over I then had time to look for more permanent employment.

The point is, take what you're given, be grateful for it, and pay what you can. Don't lose a job over a false sense of pride, as if you're better than the work required. Prioritize your life.

1. Eat well. That's what this is all about, how to eat well and live well despite your physical circumstances.

2. Your family needs a place to stay. So make the first bill that gets paid is your rent or mortgage.

3. Next, keep the utilities paid, especially a telephone. If you need to disconnect the land line in favor of a much cheaper cell, do it.

4. One car payment comes after that. Why not both? Your family may need two cars, but it certainly does not need two car payments. Sell one car along with its payment and get something cheaper or use public transportation.

5. If you can't afford the other car payment, sell it too, but you may need to get another that you have paid for in cash. You *must* get to work if you have a job, even if it's sorting automobile parts in a warehouse.

6. If you can't pay the rest, don't stress over it. Do what you can, but don't sacrifice the first three items.

My son-in-law worked for a major investment brokerage before the recent economic upheaval. He was one of the ones laid off. With no hope of being hired back, he got a job as a store clerk in a convenience store. The pay was pitiful, especially for someone with a college degree and a family to support. But he noticed something about himself. He discovered that he had hated his job working for the investment company. He found that he was far more relaxed working for the convenience store as a clerk. Interesting.

So he pursued a career in another field entirely. His parents protested that the career wasn't known for providing much of an income. He said, "Compared to what? To working as a clerk in a convenience store?"

Remember, other people's opinions are only that—opinions. They are not written in stone. You must live with your decisions, not them. Don't be too proud to accept "less than you're worth." Pride doesn't buy groceries.

If unemployed, use public transportation whenever possible. Let the transit line pay for gas. You buy a monthly pass and find work.

Staying Away from the Jim Beam Family

and Friends

Whatever you do, stay away from alcohol and other drugs. They dull the pain, but they also dull your sense of responsibility. Your priority is your family, not self-indulgence. If you can't stay away from alcohol or other drugs, get help. If you *won't* stay away, give this book to someone who takes survival seriously. If you won't stay away from self-indulgent behavior, you're not the right audience for this book.

Alcohol (or any other drug) is not a food. It dulls creativity, so it prevents productive recreation. It dulls all activity, including responding appropriately to the phone call that would have told you that of all their applicants, they want you. If you need to cut expenses, drugs have no place on your list.

A Note on Stealing

When in school, we needed to respond to a scenario about what you would do if… In the scenario, your spouse or your child is dying, and you have recently discovered that a drug company owns the cure. However, because they are the only ones with the cure, they are selling it for an exorbitant price. You are practically penniless. Do you steal the drug to save your family member, or do you let your loved one die?

In real life, there were times of no, or almost no, food. I would stop eating for a while until we were able to buy groceries again. It never occurred to me to steal groceries.

The mother of an acquaintance of mine stole groceries to feed her eight kids. She wound up in jail. Her kids were placed in a foster home where two of her girls were sexually molested. Most foster homes are not like that, but abuse does happen. Her choice to feed her family through theft nearly destroyed all of them.

If you need a more concrete illustration, remind yourself of this: If you steal anything, you are subject to arrest. Your chances of supporting your family stop. Stealing puts criminal thinking into your mindset. Once you break that barrier, the next time becomes easier.

As a breadwinner, you are the moral leader in your family. What lessons do you want to teach? What do you want to see your children doing? After watching you, and coming to the conclusion that theft is all right, they may not stop with groceries.

Consume Less – the Difference Between

Need and Want

I have a brother who is very overweight (all in our family tend to be overweight). His medicine makes him hungry all the time. However, to have any kind of a life at all, he *needs* his medicine. Unfortunately, he also believes he needs the foods he wants as much as he needs his medicine. He always serves himself the largest portion, the largest scoop of mashed potatoes with the big chunk of butter in the middle. He grabs the largest piece of pie, and at church potlucks, piles on the desserts. He also piles on the meat and starchy foods, and avoids the vegetable section during those potluck dinners. He wishes he were not so big, but he does nothing toward losing weight. When I showed him what a plate of food should look like, with half the plate in vegetables, one quarter in a *small* portion of meat, and another quarter in some kind of starchy vegetable, pasta *or* bread, he studied me as if I had just grown little green horns.

Maybe I had. I have no room to talk if I don't follow my own good advice. My problem with food is not my brother's. Because of dealing with both homelessness and hunger, I tend to look at food with a different perspective. I tend to grab it while it's available, my emotions fully convinced that it won't be there later, even while my brain reminds me that my *fat* body doesn't need that much on my plate.

So what does any of this have to do with the difference between need and want? We all have our issues with food and possessions. I can't imagine a home not filled to overflowing with books. Do I *need* all these books? Of course not, but I'm certainly willing to spend grocery money to get them. Min (my daughter, remember?) uses the library instead. I could take a lesson.

The same goes with our toys, our motorbikes and dune buggies, our many pairs of shoes and new clothing, our new furniture, computers, video games. We don't need half the things we want. Yet, somehow we convince ourselves that our next purchase is an absolute need.

Wait. Wait until you are gainfully employed before making that next purchase. *Know* the difference between a need and a want before you buy anything. Are you worried that if you wait you'll never get it at that incredibly low price? I understand, but wait anyway. Delayed gratification is a skill, and learning to reward ourselves later is a sign of maturity.

And one more piece of advice, pay cash. You don't need another bill coming in the mail.

Budgeting

One coworker was newly married. She and her husband bought a house together. Then they bought a car. They needed furniture, but they delayed the purchase of anything else until the car was paid in full. She told me that she believed in only having one credit payment in her budget, that all the rest could wait. She did have a credit card—one—that she paid on every month, but that was so that she would have excellent credit, which she did. Her husband believed the same way. Why? Because they had learned the art of budgeting.

I have read dozens of books on budgeting. None of them worked for me. They all want you to plan how much you're going to spend on clothes in a year, plan your entertainment allowance in advance, your dining out expenditure, and other expenses I've never had.

But if you have the extra, knowing what you spend on clothes, dining and entertainment in advance is vital so that you don't spend more than allowed. NEVER go over your clothing, dining and entertainment allowance. Remember the difference between need and want? You need to budget more than you need better clothes, even if you got that wonderful job. Stick to your budget. Rewrite your budget *after* you catch up your bills and after you've begun a good savings plan to weather future emergencies.

I know a woman who got a wonderful teaching position at a university. Her wardrobe was the pits, but they didn't hire her for her wardrobe. They hired her for her expertise. She upgraded her wardrobe later, not right then. Another woman, whose clothing consisted of jeans and shirts, found a job that required she wear a skirt. She washed the one skirt she owned every night and wore it each day until she could arrange for better clothing. In other words, keep to your budget.

Your budget should include your rent or house payment first. You also need to include a planned savings for unplanned emergencies, such as when the hot water heater goes out, or your tires get slashed. You will never get out of debt if you're always paying off one emergency or another. *Plan* for them. They always happen.

What does my budget look like? First you need to understand that I am writing this while unemployed and on Social Security early retirement, and that my husband is on Social Security. He used to be on Social Security Disability, but he's old enough now to be on straight Social Security. Even so, we put money aside every month into savings so that we'll have one more rent check should everything go to pieces again, or should something unexpected happen (it always does, remember?). We buy groceries, pay utilities. Our car is paid for. All my check pays the rent, and it isn't quite enough to do that, so my husband's check pays for the balance. If we need something extra, such as hairspray or underwear, those come out of the grocery budget because we have no other place for such things. Once a year, during tax return time, we either pay off a bill or buy something big that otherwise would not have been purchased at all.

2016 note: During the last four years, our finances have changed considerably. The cost of living skyrocketed, and our budget was shredded into nothing. Not wanting to pay rent for the rest of our lives, we found a small trailer that we could afford to buy. But between the house and the car payment (one car payment, remember, which was what we could afford four years ago), we found that we had very little left over. Then we had nothing left over, and then we couldn't afford the gas to get into town, and then we couldn't afford to see the doctor or buy meds, and then we couldn't afford half of our groceries. Our Social Security used to be enough. We got one doctor visit for free each year. Not anymore. I grow a garden that helps a little. I sell things at a flea market and do some bartering, which helps a little more. I don't care what the government says, lying to us, telling us things are getting better. They aren't

Pay Off Debt

This brings us to our next topic—debt. The former coworker who only has one credit card and one other bill could live comfortably on her own salary, except for the house payment. They don't have children, and aren't planning to in the near future. They are starting off on the right foot.

However, the rest of us have numerous bills that we are struggling to repay. The plan is to get our budget closer to my former coworker's: one credit card and one other bill.

To do this, choose the smallest bill, and apply all your energy to paying it off. When that one is paid off, you now have the money to apply to another bill. Use the money you are no longer applying to the first bill, and add the total to the second one, and so on.

This is the problem. If you're as strapped as most of us are these days, the second step in the plan never happens because something else does. Someone goes to the hospital, or the car breaks down, or a wind storm damages the roof, or a hundred other things. Now you have the same limited income, and another bill to pay off.

Just continue on as before, but try your level best to add one more thing to your budget—savings.

Savings

I mentioned savings briefly before. Most of us aren't taught to save, just to spend. Now it's time to learn to save too. Out of our grocery budget, we set some money aside for savings. It isn't much, but we now have enough for one month's rent, should I become unemployed again. We used to eat out more frequently. These days buying a dollar burger is eating out.

But the money we need for everything is only there when I'm working, and that hasn't been regular since I finished my very expensive education. I don't care what political garbage spews out of our "leaders'" mouths, employers don't hire people in their sixties. Since I have nearly *no* attention to detail (I'm wired very differently from most people), all my justa-jobs have never lasted more than six months.

So, back to savings again: we still devote a part of our grocery budget to savings, and supplement with food banks when we need to. A savings account is vital to any plan, if you expect the budget to work, that is.

Find Less Expensive Living Arrangements

My husband and I rent (True in 2012. Now our house will be paid off in about a year.). He is disabled, and neither of us is young. We would love to own our own home, but it's easier to have a landlord fix things. Replacing the hot water heater, for example, is not in *our* budget. And if you own a home, your budget better include a savings of several thousand dollars to fix the roof, or replace the electrical system, or any other unexpected repairs.

I worked with a man who used to make a very satisfying income—until the budget crunch. He lost his very satisfying income, and now works in a group home at less than a third of his former salary. But his bills weren't cut by two thirds. No. I asked him how he was doing, and he told me that his creditors still knew he was alive. They call regularly to make sure. Nice of them.

So what does he do? He rents out a couple of bedrooms to make his house payment, and everyone else needs to stand in line.

What do the rest of us do? Find cheaper housing. We do have choices. We can tough out our house payment, like my friend, or we can sell the place, even if it's at a loss, and move. But renting isn't always cheaper. Check your local market. Know the rent prices, or the housing prices before you make this step. You could be in for a real, not very pleasant, surprise.

2016 note: The cost of housing has skyrocketed again. And rent is expensive. I don't know where this is headed, but it doesn't look good.

If at all possible do not live in a motel. The monthly price for a motel room is often higher than rent. Plus, you need to rent a storage unit for the rest of your stuff, unless you want to sell off everything and start from scratch.

You can also be homeless. Homelessness does not usually happen by choice. Living in your car or a shelter while going to work or looking for work is a lousy way to live.

You can choose to camp out for the summer until things turn around. We did. Once. Except things never turned around very well. We ended up living with another family for seven months until we could afford to move into our own place.

Sometimes your choices are limited. But start to plan and explore your options NOW, before things get worse. One certainty—things can always get worse. Take as much control as you can before they do.

And don't forget to pray. *Don't* pray, "Oh, God!" Hear the desperate sound of that prayer?

Instead pray, "Most holy and wonderful God…" Spend some time here. Know WHO you are praying to. Know the love and power that surrounds your creator. Explore the fact that you were created out of amazing love, that it was not an accident that you were born.

Neither was it an accident that you are in these dire circumstances. "And we know that in all things, **God works** for the good of those who love him and are called according to his purpose" (Romans 8:28 NIV). The subject in the original Greek is "God." The verb is "works." "God works." He is still working, and he has not abandoned you, no matter how you feel.

Chapter 4

Buying, Selling, Trading

Buy now—pay later. That's the trouble. We buy and buy with little regard for the future, until the future is upon us and we're so far in debt we have no idea how to dig out. A couple of generations ago, people put back their money "for a rainy day." They never considered buying *without* money. But here we are, the future upon us, with our sense of responsibility somewhere in left field, buying lottery tickets for that chance to get out of debt.

I have no trouble with a person buying *one* lottery ticket, especially if the jackpot is over 100 million. However, the other day I heard about a woman who "only" spent a few hundred dollars each payday on lottery tickets. Only? Her sense of responsibility is in left field. If she put that same couple of hundred dollars each payday in a savings account, she would have the needed nest egg for the day her job died, or some other emergency appeared.

Life is full of emergencies. Instead of buy now and pay later, we need to readjust our thinking to plan now and don't buy until we can afford to pay cash. The car will get hit, or the dog will need emergency surgery, or you will, or a hundred other things that can go wrong.

During one six-month period, our daughter needed to be put in private school (I won't go into the reasons.). The same daughter needed physical therapy because her bones grew faster than her muscles. Our sister-in-law used our phone to make $600 of long-distance calls that she never intended to reimburse. During that time we experienced two other emergencies, one including a business that failed. By the end of the six-month period we had literally lost everything, our business, our home. Everything. We found ourselves homeless. Life happens.

Now, I'm not saying the same things will happen to you. Instead, I'm saying that if you don't plan for the future and *life happens*, what will your new toy or hobby, or that lottery ticket money that should have gone into savings, contribute?

Right. Nothing. So plan now, buy later, when you have the cash.

Garage Sales, Second-Hand Stores

and On Sale

But there does come a time when you must buy something. One huge advantage of living in a country where so many people overbuy is that you can get quality items for very low prices when they have to get rid of them. We purchased our washer and dryer used, but in excellent condition. We purchased our lawnmower for five dollars at a garage sale four years ago, and it's still running well. It's not a necessity, but I found a lovely Asian-style painting that works very well in our dining room. Be choosey. At garage sale prices you can afford to be.

Another place to look for good buys are at second-hand places. Habitat For Humanity stores have items for your home at very good prices, including furniture, floor tiles, bathroom fixtures, plumbing and paneling. At second hand clothing stores, you can find a wide selection of good clothing for a fraction of the cost, especially when they're designer clothing.

Regardless, if you do need to buy something new, try to get it on sale. I have purchased quality sandals for just a few dollars at a good shop because they were on sale. Check flyers, coupons and prices before you buy anything. Make your dollars count. Make them work for you, not against you.

Trading

Trading is nearly a lost art in our country. Some communities have publications that have a section on trading. You can also advertise in some public places like laundromats and college bulletin boards. There are communities where the art of trading is alive a well. We used to live in such a community. Only a few people had money, so trading had become a way of life. We traded for both goods and services in that community. Do you do something very well? Do you speak French, for example? Could you trade a certain number of conversational French lessons to the daughter of a plumber to get your faucet fixed? Do you make excellent afghans? Could you trade an afghan for a lube job? If you plan to do some trading, make sure that what you're offering is top quality, especially when trading for services.

Odd Jobbing

During a time of partial employment, I cleaned houses for extra money. The extra money wasn't extra at all, of course, but a bit of income to pay on some of the bills that weren't getting paid at all. Just about anything can be an odd job. Usually you're providing a service that most people wouldn't want to do in the first place, like trimming hedges. Odd jobbing is kind of like trading, in that you're trading a service for cash, but you could odd job for an item or another service as well. Ask around. Someone may need exactly what you offer.

Chapter 5

Scratch – Make Something

Not everything needs to be purchased. I taught myself how to both knit and crochet. Following my example, my daughter taught herself how to sew. Everything that you are able to do for yourself is something you don't need to buy. Will you be making all your own clothes and blankets, tablecloths and napkins? Probably not, but there comes a sense of accomplishment that only comes from making something yourself.

Blankets

You can knit and crochet afghans. You can also recycle old blankets by backing the blanket with an old sheet and topping it with a pieced-together quilt top you made yourself. You don't need to quilt it unless you want to. The easiest way to make a quilt is by tying.

Place old sheet on the floor, print side down.

Put your blanket on top and pin together.

Baste (needle and thread in long in-and-out stitches) from center outward to corners first, then to edges. This is to hold both pieces together.

Turn over. Now the blanket is on the floor and the print side is up.

Place the quilt top, outside down, on top of the basted sheet. Pin on three sides.

Sew the three sides together on a sewing machine. Trim margin to less than $\frac{1}{2}$ inch. Snip the corners off almost to the stitching.

Turn inside out, so that the outside of the sheet and the quilt top are on the outside and the blanket is in the middle. Remove basting from back side.

Pin, then baste through all three layers so that the top doesn't slip away from the bottom when you stitch up the unfinished side.

Tuck in the edges of the unfinished side and pin.

Sew unfinished edge.

Do not remove basting yet.

With yarn and tapestry needle or with string and needle, bring thread through all three layers and then back around to the front. Tie ends together and snip thread.

These ties are what makes a tied quilt. Dot with ties across whole blanket.

Remove basting threads.

Note: This whole project can be done by hand, without a sewing machine, provided you keep your stitches small. For those who stitch by hand, there are several kinds of stitches people use. My mother-in-law used a cross stitch, which was pretty as well as sturdy. My grandmother used a back stitch, which is exceptional for making tight seams. But a simple in and out stitch, or running stitch, if kept small, will work fine for quilts. Our ancestors who moved west from the great eastern cities didn't have sewing machines because they didn't have electricity. But they did have old clothes that were hardly more than rags which became the filling for their quilts. They used what they had. Even rugged cowboys were known to take a needle and thread to patch up a torn garment and stitch together a quilt for those cold nights on the open prairie.

Bags

Anymore you can buy shopping bags with the store's logo on it. But if you go to the fabric store and look at their ends and pieces, you can buy thick upholstery fabric for pennies on the dollar. This fabric makes excellent bags. Just remember that the heavier the fabric, the thicker your needle and the stronger your thread needs to be.

Napkins

In this country people spend a small fortune on paper products, killing far too many trees in the process. You can be economical and ecologically sensible all at the same time!

Again, go to a fabric store and look for the ends and pieces of fabric.

This time select a lightweight swatch of cloth. Fold it in half and half again and again until it is slightly larger than the napkins you want, the cut along the folds. Hem up all four ends, either by hand or by machine, and you have washable napkins (provided, of course, you purchased washable fabric). This is also a time when you can get fancy and learn some embroidery. The edges can be sewn in brightly colored embroidery thread in a variety of stitches, cross stitches, blanket stitches, or even a feather stitch.

No time? Do you spend an hour watching TV? That's when I do my needlework, during that hour of TV time. Is it easier to buy paper towels and paper napkins? Of course, but it's also more expensive.

Knitting a Winter Scarf

A Garter Stitch Scarf

This is a very easy knitting pattern for a garter stitch scarf knit from side to side. Great knitting pattern for beginners because you knit every row!

Materials:
Size 15 US (10 mm) circular needles 26" or longer
2 balls (55 yards/50 grams) yarn in one color
1 ball yarn (120 yards/50 grams) in another color
Gauge:
Not vital-approximately 7 sts=4"
Remember this will be the length because you are knitting from side to side and the number of sts you CO (cast over) is the length, not the width

Size:
Approximately 8" wide x 60" long

Instructions:
Scarf is knit with one strand of one color and one strand of another color held together throughout.

Loosely CO 100 sts.
Knit every row until you are almost out yarn.
BO (bind over) loosely.

Gently pull on both sides of the scarf. The scarf will be quite elastic.

Crocheting a Winter Scarf

This scarf pattern is worked in 5ply wool using a 5.00mm crochet hook. The stitches used are chain, trebles, puff stitch (draw up 3 loops only). The edges are finished with fringing. For a different option, you might like to make tassels instead of fringing.

Materials: Depending on the length of the scarf you require, 200 – 300 grams 5ply wool, 5.00mm crochet hook.

Tension: 1st 5 rows = Approximately 5cm [2ins]

Measurements: Approximately 138cm [55ins] long, 22.5cm [9ins] wide.

CROCHET SCARF PATTERN

Begin by working 37 chain.

1st Row: Work 1tr into 4th ch from hook, 1tr into each ch to end, 3ch, turn.

2nd Row: Work 1tr into each tr to end, finishing with 1tr into top of 1st 3ch st., 3ch turn.

3rd Row: As 2nd Row.

4th Row: Work 3ch, *miss next st, work 1 puff st into next tr, 2ch, repeat from * to end of row finishing with 1ch after last puff st, 1tr into top of 3ch, 3ch turn.

5th Row: Work 3ch, *1tr into puff st, 1tr into sp, repeat from* finishing with 1tr in last st, 3ch, turn.

These 5 rows form the pattern. Continue in this manner until scarf reaches desired length, finishing with 3 rows of tr.

Make fringing with 4 strands of wool [more if you wish], and attach them between the first and second stitch and every alternate stitch space at both ends of your crochet scarf.

Scratch – Grow Something

Unlike our grandparents, most of us now live in cities. During the Depression, which this crisis is being compared to, my father's family lived on a farm and grew all their own food. Even many of those in cities grew backyard gardens and sometimes had chickens.

That's not our world. But it's possible to grow something, even in a city apartment. By growing something, I'm talking about food, not pretty plants. Remember, this book is dedicated to survival, which makes most potted plants luxuries, not necessities.

What can grow in a city apartment? And what if you have no good sunlight coming in your windows? To the second question, use fluorescent grow lights in your light fixtures. You'll save money, and have artificial sunlight filling your home.

But what grows in an apartment? If you have a balcony or one sunny window you can grow a number of things in hanging baskets, such as certain hybrid cherry tomatoes or strawberries. If you have a nice well-lit corner, you can try a dwarf citrus or avocado tree. If you're lucky enough to have a patio, you can do quite a bit with potted gardens. And if you're even luckier with a patch of yard, you can grow a bit of a garden.

If you have very limited space, you can still grow sprouts which are great on sandwiches in the place of lettuce, and much more nutritious. They're also good in salads. Just sprouts, you ask? Remember, everything you grow yourself is something you don't need to buy. And sprout seeds explode in nutritious value when they're sprouted. Be adventurous. Grow radish seeds, mung bean seeds, alfalfa seeds. Just remember to buy the seeds at a health food store so that you're not sprouting treated seeds meant for gardens. Those seeds are *not* good for you at all!

I got married right out of high school after I turned eighteen. I would have married at seventeen, but my parents refused to sign for me. My marriage has lasted over fifty years, so the story of those who marry young divorce early is not necessarily true. But as a result, we've never been wealthy. My husband was a blue-collar worker before his disability and never wanted to be anything else. But I always had higher aspirations. I wanted a degree and a profession. If I couldn't have them, I wanted to stay home and take care of my babies.

Even so, I kept trying to go to school. One of those times I attended Ft. Lewis College in Durango. I can't explain to you how broke we were. Because we couldn't afford Durango prices, we lived in Pagosa Springs, which isn't much better. Wages were minimum and prices are comparable to Denver. We rented a tinny mobile home with poor insulation. Although summers are nice, winters in Pagosa Springs are brutal. We kept our house around fifty-five degrees to save on propane, but even so couldn't afford the price of propane. Once we had to choose between buying groceries or buying propane. I, who have always been chunky, lost a lot of weight that year. A lady at church commented on how much weight I lost, and I made a joke of it, saying, "Well, when there's no food, I don't eat. Works every time."

This is what I ate. I skipped breakfast and drove to school. Around 10:00 I ate an apple that I brought with me. About noon I ate a cheese sandwich (commodity cheese provided by the USDA). On the sandwich was a huge layer of sprouts which we grew in the kitchen in jars. Pagosa winters are *very* long, and vegetables *very* pricey. I returned home somewhere between 6pm and 8pm. At that time I ate supper with my family. We sometimes ate stew with real meat. Often we ate beans and tortillas or beans and cornbread. We bought one-hundred pound bags of both potatoes and beans which lasted most of the winter for the six of us (my husband, myself, three children and a disabled brother).

My diet kept me healthy that horrible year, even if the number of calories was slim. The key is to always look for quality, especially when you can't afford quantity. Eat brown bread, fresh fruits and vegetables whenever possible and a complete protein at every meal. Make whatever you can afford be as nutritious as possible. Grow something so that you eat better. Sprouts are a great survival food!

Apartment Gardening

Just because you live in an apartment doesn't mean you can't garden. If you have a window that lets in sunlight, use it. If you have a patio, use it. If you have none of the above, get fluorescent grow lights and use those. If you have a brown thumb, skip this chapter. Plants are alive, and must be cared for as growing, living, breathing things.

Growing Sprouts

If you're new to eating sprouts, don't make too much at first. Once you get the hang of it, you can start another jar three days after you start the first jar. The next jars will be ready after you finish eating the first batch.

The most important point: when you strain seeds, make sure that they're really strained. Sprouting is remarkable; all you need are the seeds and water. But add too much water and the seeds may rot. Nevertheless, it's pretty difficult to make the seeds rot, as long as you follow the steps carefully.

Go to your health food store for the seeds. NEVER buy garden seeds for sprouting. They have been treated and are NOT good for you. Choose from among: alfalfa, clover, mung beans, lentil, garbanzo, wheat berries and rye.

Soak the Seeds

Any time you cook with seeds or beans, it's a good practice to inspect them before you go any further. Take the portion of seeds or beans, and pour them out onto a large plate, serving dish, or baking sheet. Push the seeds on one side of the dish, and inspect them for broken or withered seeds, and small stones or lumps of dirt. (If you have kids, this a good time to bring them into the act.) After they're sorted, pour them into a strainer and give them a good rinse.

Pour the rinsed seeds into the jar.

Cover them with adequate water—a few inches above the level of the seeds. Let the seeds soak overnight. Medium-sized seeds should be soaked 8-12 hours, and large beans and nuts can soak for 12-24 hours.

Note: Water, water everywhere...but it's not always fit to drink. Or for that matter, grow sprouts with. Many municipal water supplies around the world have been contaminated by industrial and agricultural pollutants. If you soak the seeds in that water, your sprouts may absorb those pollutants and pass them on to you. Eating sprouts made in contaminated water may have an adverse health affect over time, so consider using filtered or spring water for sprouting.

Strain

Next morning, cover the mouth of the jar with cheesecloth, and fasten with a rubber band. Turn over the jar in the sink. The cheesecloth acts as a strainer, holding in the seeds and letting out the water. If you're using the bowl method, use the strainer to strain out the soaking water and rinse the seeds. Let it drain all day.

Note: Some people save this soaking water. It contains valuable nutrients that you can mix into a health shake with other ingredients like soup, fruit and yogurt. Or use it for your houseplants—they'll be very grateful.

Shake the jar (or strainer) a few times to remove all of the water from last night's soak.

Rinse: Fill up with water, and again drain out the water, ending with a few hearty shakes. Hold the jar up to the light; the seeds should be mostly dry. If there's too much water left in the jar, the seeds may rot over the next few days. But if you're even slightly careful to drain the seeds, that probably won't happen.

To ensure complete drainage, some folks store the jar upside-down in a glass baking dish or plastic tub. Rest the jar on the side of the dish, or up against the wall--any excess water drains out, without any more attention from you.

Repeat: On the evening of the same day, you'll repeat the rinsing process. You'll continue this morning and evening rinsing for 4 or 5 days (in warm climates, figure a day or two less than that). If you're feeling particularly keen on sprouting, you can rinse it a third time at noon.

Watch for the growth: you'll see green leaves sprouting on seeds, and white shoots on beans, nuts, and grains.

Harvest: After four or five days, the sprouts will reach their peak of flavor and nutritional value. Give them a final rinse; drain with a hearty shake. Now they're ready to be prepared and devoured by the hungry masses.

So many uses! Your biggest problem with sprouting is choosing among these alternatives:

- Add to salads and sandwiches, and as a garnish on soups.
- Puree seeds and beans to make a fantastic sandwich spread or vegetable dip. For flavors, try adding tahini, lemon, and garlic for a middle Eastern flair; or fresh tomato and basil for a Mediterranean touch.
- Cook bean sprouts: lightly stir-fry them with other vegetables, or add to other recipes like veggie burgers. Also very good when steamed with shredded carrot and cabbage.

Sprouted grains are a bit trickier to use. They're often ground up and baked at low temperatures (220 degrees) to make bread, or added to recipes like casseroles.

Outdoor Gardening

Not all outdoor gardens are created equal. I rent my home, so I can't just dig up my landlord's property. Furthermore, practically the whole back yard is concrete. So I do quite a bit of container gardening.

But if you're lucky and you have some actual land, all gardening takes is water, seed and hard work.

Min, my daughter, lives in Phoenix. She has seen me grow things her whole life, so she decided to give it a try. She started some cucumbers, but squash beetles got the flowers, so no fruit grew. Because it was so hot, the lettuce and radishes bolted, meaning instead of produce they produced seeds. Her two young sons watched their mother go through these strange activities. She was growing food, she explained.

Finally she harvested a carrot, a skinny little thing that fit too neatly in the palm of his hand. "We grew this carrot," she told him.

He looked at the carrot and said, "Hello, my carrot!"

If you want to grow tomatoes from seed, choose a seed that produces the fruit you want. In Pagosa Springs, for example, I purchased sub-arctic tomato seeds. I planted them indoors in February, and put out the flowering plants in June. My garden was heavy with green fruit by the end of July. Unfortunately on August 1st we had a snowstorm, and I had to harvest my whole crop.

We ate fried green tomatoes. I canned jars of green tomato relish. And I let some of them ripen. That Thanksgiving we ate fresh, home-grown tomatoes for dinner.

If you want to do some serious gardening, I suggest you buy yourself a book. This book is only meant to be an overview of what you can do, and to let you know that you, like your crops, can bloom where you're planted.

Scratch – Mending and Making Do

I have sewn patches on jeans, mended pajamas, shortened hems, lengthened hems, made a baby's play blanket from pieces of clothing (full of pockets and things that tied, buttoned and zipped. Both the baby and the mother loved it.), re-sewn seams, and replaced zippers. When you have no money, you learn to make what you have work for you.

The Fine Art of Mending

I hate mending. Things will remain in the mending pile for years before I'll get to them. I want to create beautiful things, like hand-crocheted rugs and beautiful prom dresses and western shirts. I hate sewing on buttons, mending seams, and repairing pockets. But I've done all of it.

Machine Sewing

A sewing machine is a craftsman's tool. I have made wedding dresses, western shirts, costumes and prom dresses on my machine. I have designed clothing and remade clothing on one. But I didn't start out knowing how to sew. Just like any tool, I needed to learn how to use it. My first machine was a used one I bought for $5. Dear! What an ancient machine that was!

I practiced by making clothing for my kids. Those poor kids! They were so proud of my creations, but I could see every mistake.

Anyway, I have also used my sewing machine to recover my couch as well as using it to make a number of other household items.

Curtains

We moved around a lot. No matter what curtains you buy for your home, they often don't fit the next one. So either you have a lot of unwanted fabric, or you learn to sew your curtains. I learned to sew them.

However, I couldn't always afford the necessary fabric. So I used old sheets. You can get old sheets in garage sales, or by wearing out the bottom sheet. The top sheet can be used for a number of things, including curtains. Sometimes you can get sheets on sale for less than the fabric would cost in a fabric store.

Café curtains are the easiest to make. You need a short length for the top part, and a longer one for the bottom. Measure your window. You want twice (or almost twice) the width of the window so it will gather nicely. The top, or valance, is a single piece. Machine hem the fabric on all four sides. Fold the top over about two inches. About a half inch from the top of your curtain you want to put in a little seam. This will ruffle nicely when you gather it across your curtain rod. Then, looking at the back side of your curtain, you want to sew along the same line as the tiny hem you sewed all the way around the fabric. The gap between the half-inch top seam and the bottom will hold your curtain rod.

Do the same with your bottom piece, except remember that it is in two pieces so that you can open it from the center. If you want a ruffle along the bottom you'll need more fabric. This can be the same or contrasting, your choice.

I keep saying I'm going to crochet myself some curtains. Maybe someday I will.

Tablecloths and Napkins

This is kind of like making curtains, except that if you want something dressy, you probably ought to learn how to embroider. There are a few of us still around who like to embroider. Take a chance. Maybe you're also one of them.

I ought to crochet edgings on my napkins too.

Hand Sewing

Hand sewing is an art. I never mastered it. But my mother-in-law made a whole dress by hand sewing it.

I never had that kind of patience. Still, it's possible. It's a lot slower, but if stitching fabric by hand relaxes you, by all means, do it. There is a certain amount of joy in finishing something you started by hand. I just don't understand how I can get so much pleasure from embroidering something and totally resist hand sewing.

Blankets

We already had one chapter on making blankets. But this chapter is on mending, so do what you can with your sewing machine or by hand stitching, to give your blanket another life. You can also patch blankets.

My mother crocheted a lovely white bedspread. That sounds like a lot more fun!

Mending Socks

My advice is—don't! If the heel is worn out, the rest will soon follow. But if you MUST have those socks, you can do an in and out stitch, or a basket weave across the worn spot. The toe? Just sew it up if you can. And then next payday, buy yourself another pair of socks.

When my father went into the service, he came home and announced to his mother that in the Army they throw away worn socks. Grandmother was appalled. How wasteful! But an army marches on its feet, and once a sock begins wearing out, it isn't much good after that.

Throw away your worn socks. Consider good socks an investment like good food.

Chapter 6

Christmas and Other Costly Holidays

One rule of thumb, no matter what the holiday, never spend more than you'll be able to pay back. I know people who put everything on credit cards, and then spend years paying on the card. Not smart.

Christmas Decorations

Buy your Christmas decorations at the end of the year, *after* Christmas. So what if your tree is bare the first year? You'll have lots of decorations for your next Christmas. Besides, you could make some, right? One friend covered her tree in bows!

One Christmas we had no money for either a tree or decorations. We had some garland and a lot of paper chains and things that the kids had made, but nothing nice. And certainly no money for a tree. What to do? I took one blank wall, cut up some wrapping paper in tree-branch shapes and taped them to the wall. Then I took some of the decorations that we did have and also taped them to the wall. We had our Wallflower Christmas Tree. The gifts fit under it nicely, but it didn't light up very well.

Christmas Gifts

Do what you can. Just don't go into debt. Debt is a killer and it often lasts far longer than the Christmas you purchased. There are some things you can make. And there are some creative ways to give gifts. You can give something you already own, something you repaired like new.

Or you can wrap up a promise. For example, you can make coupons, like "This coupon is good for one car wash provided by me when the weather turns nice."

You can offer free babysitting, or a candlelit dinner. You can give a massage or a shampoo. Your imagination is the limit. I used to call my imagination my Magic Nation. It is. It's the location of where all great ideas originate, and it's truly magic.

But if you have no imagination, oh, well…

Regifting

Some people would never regift if their lives depended on it. So they say. But if your survival really does depend on it, you might reconsider. Besides, what newlywed needs three toasters? Did Aunt Mabel give you a hand-knit sweater that you wouldn't put on your dog? Maybe Uncle Henry would love that hand-knitted sweater. Think about it and don't be selfish. If you have an overabundance, it's time to share.

I do know a friend, though, who has a regifting planner, so she knows where her gifts came from and who might notice that it was indeed Aunt Mabel who had made the sweater. We don't want to embarrass someone. Neither do we want to insult them. So be careful.

Chapter 7

Last Is First – Spiritual Direction

Love means to love that which is unlovable,

or it is no virtue at all;

forgiving means to pardon that which is unpardonable,

or it is no virtue at all—

and to hope means hoping when things are hopeless,

or it is no virtue at all.

G.K. Chesterton

You may own nothing, but you are very, very rich. You are rich in God's love. You are rich in His mercy. You are rich in a future that lasts forever.

There was a young Moslem woman who, through friends at school, found Jesus. She was a very wealthy woman who had never lacked for a physical thing. She was her father's darling, and her mother's joy, but when she found Jesus, she realized that in salvation, she had everything. All the physical things were only that—things.

Needless to say, her family was furious. Her father sent people after her to change her mind. She did not. He encouraged her friends to change her mind. She did not. Finally, sore at heart, he had her thrown into prison where she was beaten and tortured. Then he came to her, to change her mind.

He said, "Will you throw all of your life away for this fantasy? Will you throw away your riches, your family, your community, everything?"

She replied, "I have had everything, but it is nothing. I now have everything, and it is far more than you can give."

He had her put to death.

Most of us worship a god that is too small. This god is the Everything-Will-All-Turn-Out-All-Right god, but it is such a superficial deity. Sometimes nothing works out well. Then where do we go? To whom do we turn? Where is that god when nothing works out?

We used to live in Pagosa Springs where winter lasts eight months out of the year. It is a hard life for those who have little. A waitress once said, "All summer I do without so that all winter I can....do without."

During times like those, your faith needs to be much larger than the ordinary.

While we lived in Pagosa Springs, I attended Ft. Lewis College in Durango. But our car, my transportation to drive the sixty miles to Durango, died. So I hitchhiked. It was not a safe decision, but at the time I had little choice.

One night my ride from Durango could only take me as far as Turkey Creek. He asked if this would be all right. I told him it was, because I would not ask more of him than he was willing to give.

But it was a *very* dark night, with no moon. There were no lights, no farm or ranch lights, no businesses, nothing. It was so dark I couldn't see my feet on the pavement. I was scared.

Then a truck drove up. The truck was filled with young men. Honestly, I couldn't see that there was anywhere to sit. And as the truck door opened, an empty pop can bounced out. It wasn't a beer can, but I still didn't feel safe.

"No, I told them. I'm all right. I don't really live far from here."

That was a lie. My home was still twenty miles away.

There was no other traffic. I was convinced I had just made the worst decision of my life. And I was really scared now. It was eight o'clock at night, with no one out and about. I began praying.

God said, "Look up."

So I looked up. And I saw the most amazing starry night. It was so dark that I could actually see the colors of the stars, red ones and blue ones, yellow, green and white, all shining like tiny Christmas tree lights.

"If I can make all of this," God said, "I can certainly protect you."

Now, I don't usually hear the voice of God, but this was in the context of prayer, and every once in a while I recognize that quiet voice. I knew I was safe.

A few minutes later another vehicle drove up, a car with two women in the front seat. They had been shopping in Durango and wanted to know if they could take me home. They drove me right to my doorstep.

You are rich. And it's about time you start sharing your wealth.

Volunteer

Now why would I put in a section on volunteering? Does it bring in any money? Does volunteering pay the bills, or keep the collectors off the phone?

It's because it does nothing of monetary value that I suggest it. Instead, it gets you out of yourself and out of your problems and takes you into another world. You owe people for your existence. You do! When one of us hurts, we all hurt, and now it's time for you to understand the hurts of others. You owe them your time and attention. You need to know *why* we take care of those who cannot care for themselves. You need to understand problems outside of your own.

And you need to know that you have some power to help relieve their suffering. You need to help give them voice, a way to tell the world that they're out there. You need to not turn your back like so many others do. By helping others you empower yourself with more than money. You receive gifts that cannot be taken away, even after death. And you learn the purpose and power of gratitude.

Expectations and Gratitude

Because I attend church regularly, I hear more than a few prayer requests. Most of the requests regard health. People get sick and need prayer. People get a terminal disease and want healing. Pets get sick, but because Dad lost his job and Mom's job won't support the whole family, children ask for help for their dog or cat.

The next most common request used to be for traveling mercies for those taking vacations or visiting relatives across the mountain. But lately employment stepped up to the number two slot. Either a family member just lost a job, or the income got cut and no overtime can be allowed. I saw a sign recently where a single-owner business only stayed open four hours a day. They were a carpet-installing company. They provided a phone number for after-hours access. My guess is that in order to keep his business open at all, the owner found another job. Life sometimes stinks.

In this country we expect a certain level of both spiritual and physical care. We don't expect to go hungry. We protest against the slightest inconvenience. We must have our programming and our games. We spend more money on frivolous desires that most of those in the world can even earn.

And when our desires are thwarted, we rail against God.

During most of the world's history, the poor were *really* poor, and the chance to be otherwise almost non-existent. *Most* of the world fell into the desperately poor category. Yet the Psalms sing to us of praising God for his many blessings. The blessings, however, focused on the glory of God and his faithfulness in providing things like mountainous beauty, rainy seasons, forgiveness and mercy. Their expectations were different. They expected to have to wait for the harvest. They expected inclement weather and scorching sun. When something else happened, like a bumper crop, that was called a blessing. Shade was called a blessing.

God's mercy was, still is, called a blessing.

Let me repeat that: God's mercy is called a blessing.

Why? Because God doesn't owe us anything, certainly not mercy.

Well, if we compare our works to the goodness, or lack of goodness, found in others, we probably fare well. We control our anger. We give to charities. We sing in choir. We tithe, or at least give a little on Sundays.

We volunteer at the homeless shelter. We bake cookies and give them away. We don't lie, steal, cuss or kill, even though the thoughts cross our minds.

But if we compare our actions to a perfect God, we always come up short. Furthermore, God allows no imperfection near him. In God's presence, our petty desires, our trivial wants that we rail against God as our right, are both sinful and disrespectful. We have done far too little to earn the attention of the most holy and perfect God. Our greed, our sharp words, ungracious thoughts and acts of malice, the tiny slips of misdirection that come out of our mouths, are all sin. The penalty for sin has never changed. It has always been death and eternal separation from God. We will die. We cannot fix that part.

Thank God our lives don't end there! Instead, God gives us another way to access him. In God is life. He created life because he loves it. He created us because he loves us, and he wants an eternal relationship with us. But the price for sin still needed to be paid. The second part, the eternal piece, can be fixed. He made that possible so that the people he loves can still spend eternity with him. He is the One who cares for us more than we can either understand or imagine. We can accept God's mercy and forgiveness through Jesus.

Jesus never sinned. He never earned the penalty of death. He could have just gone home and never died. But someone needed to pay the price. Even if we died for ourselves, we still could do nothing to earn an eternal relationship with the Father. Sin is an eternal blot on our record. Jesus, with not even a spec on his record, took all the charges against us and became black with everyone's blots and specs. He paid *our* penalty, even though he never needed to. He conquered sin.

Then he did something else extraordinary. He rose, conquering death itself. What did this death look like? After Jesus died and rose, Thomas touched him, so he was physical. He ate fish, so he was not stone but flesh. But he was also glorified, a spiritual *and* physical being. Accepting

Jesus' sacrifice restores each one of us to our intended structure. Not only is access to the Father reestablished, but so are our purposes with each other. We will no longer be alone. We will truly be one with each other, individual, unique, yet aware of each other in a way I'm sure I cannot define while in this very limited form.

Jesus said if you have two coats, give one away to the one who has none. We are to *live* like that.

Death and Dying

What terrifies you? Are you afraid of losing your house, your possessions, your health, your ability to earn a living, of death?

Let's look at the worst that could happen. Look your monster straight in the eye. It goes something like this:

I hate being unemployed. It's more than simply needing to tighten our belts, not going out, cutting the grocery budget, not answering the phone because of bill collectors, and so on. It's a sin called Worry. Worry is born of fear. I've been both hungry and homeless, so I know what those two things feel like. I've had to do without medication because I couldn't afford it. I've not gone to doctors for the same reason. I've walked for miles because I couldn't afford either gas or public transportation. What am I afraid of? All of it.

Is the bottom line death? Well, no. I'm not really afraid of death. For a Christian, death is a reward. No, what I'm afraid of is the *process* of death, the getting there. I'm the primary breadwinner. My husband is disabled. So I worry that I might not be able to keep him safe. I worry that if we lose our home we'll have to live on the streets, and he wouldn't survive long. I'm afraid of feeling guilty I'm afraid I will believe there was something unfinished that I should have done and didn't do. I'm afraid that the whole burden is all on me.

But what worry really does is paralyze me. I can't function. I go over the budget a hundred times and nothing different happens. Out of desperation I apply at every job out there, whether I can do the work or not. Because I interview well, I have received some of those jobs only to lose them six months later. Then I needed to face my fears all over again.

Recently I began to ask myself one big question. What is the worst that could happen?

Well, we could lose our home. We would then need to live in a shelter or on the streets. The pets would go to a shelter. The tropical fish would go down the drain. My husband might not get his medication, and he would get even sicker. I would have even more difficulty finding work while living at a shelter. And my husband would die.

As I look at this I am noticing several things, but the one that strikes me the hardest is losing my husband of fifty-plus years. As I said before, I'm not afraid of death, but of the *process* of dying. The fact is, I can do *nothing* to keep my husband from dying. With medication, I can delay his death by a number of years, but eventually he is going to die anyway. When he dies, he will be home with his Maker, and be rewarded. Although I want to delay his death, it is inevitable. As is mine.

It seems to me, then, that the problem is more of a spiritual problem than it is a physical one. Everyone dies. People grieve. So will I someday, and I better come to terms with it. Coming to terms with grief does not lessen the impact of the grief. Instead, I learn to rely on my Lord for all the things in my life, both great and small. I learn to ask for eternal things like courage, compassion and wisdom, and as I build my character on a firm foundation of faith, I will be more able to look this monster in the eye and be healed from the sin of worry.

Worry does something else. Worry takes our mind off others and off our Lord, and places our attention inside ourselves. We see nothing else. We do not see our loved ones trying to reach out to us. We miss our Lord's direction. We even miss opportunities that would lessen the impact of our situation. Worry puts our focus in the wrong place, making the rest of the world, where we should be looking, out of focus.

There was a woman who survived the Holocaust. She had no control during that time in her life. It was not her fault that she was placed in the middle of that horror, and it was not her fault that she survived. But ever afterwards, she lived her life as if waiting for the other shoe to drop. No matter how many times she was blessed, she firmly believed that somehow it would all be taken away again.

I'm not judging her. I'm just sorry she chose that reaction, because she missed out on the rest of her life. In her mind, she never got out of that horror. I don't want to live inside the bad times. No matter what happens, I want to experience joy, have hope, laugh and love.

Wherever you are, look for joy and hope, laugh and love. Get out of yourself so that you don't miss out on the important parts of living. This life is only temporary anyway. There are many more things to look at than your own problems. As for my husband, I hope that I can be there as he dies so that he can see love and hope, joy and laughter, and go home with those things on his mind.

Lord, grant us strength and courage to face the future, whatever it may hold. And fill our hearts and minds with your presence.

Blessings,

Patricia Renard Scholes

Other Books by Patricia Renard Scholes

Herbal/Survival:
Surviving Hard Times – A Livingbook
Healing Herbs from Your Kitchen
Bountiful Backyard – A Willowbark Tea Wildcrafting Introduction
(available soon)
A Willowbark Tea Herbal Garden
(available soon)
39 Healthy Teas You Can Make at Home
30 Superfoods – Plan Your Diet from These Foods, Get Healthy and Stay
Healthy

Lorekeeper of the Tapestry series
Her Darkest Beauty
Steps of the Dance
Her Dark Inheritance

Song of the Lorekeeper Series
Into Darkness
Counterweave
New Threads
Broken Thread

Bible Study
I AM – The Words Jesus Said About Himself

Co-published with Christopher Renard:
The Fox and Abd al-Qadir, My March Toward Freedom,
as told by a prisoner of the Third Jihad

About the Author

When her husband became disabled, Patricia decided to return to school. She attended Denver Seminary with the intention of pastoring a church somewhere. But after she graduated the economy changed and she could not pursue her career.

Patricia now works from home as a free-lance writer. She cooks, gardens, sews, crochets, and embroiders. She still has her loving husband, a dog, two cats, and some tropical fish. She still has her loving husband.

Together they take foster kids into their home.

She writes from her own experiences and learns from the experiences of others. You may learn more about Patricia on her web: www.willowbarktea.com. Your comments are welcome.